Tractor

You can re...

If you require help p...

Annabel Savery

W

FRANKLIN WATTS
LONDON•SYDNEY

This edition 2013

First published in 2009 by
Franklin Watts
338 Euston Road
London NW1 3BH

Franklin Watts Australia
Level 17/207 Kent Street
Sydney NSW 2000

ISBN: 978 1 4451 1745 4

Dewey classification number: 629.2'252

A CIP catalogue record for this book is available
from the British Library.

Planning and production by Discovery Books Limited
Managing editor: Rachel Tisdale
Editor: Annabel Savery
Designer: Ian Winton

Acknowledgments: Case IH: pp. 4, 6, 7, 13 top, 20, 23, 30; Challenger/AGCO Audio
Visual Department: p. 9; Fendt: pp. cover main, 20 top, 27 top; Discovery Photo
Library: p. 16 (Chris Fairclough); Grimme: p. 21 bottom; Hardi International: p. 19;
Istockphoto.com: p. 18 (Tomasz Szymanski); Massey Ferguson: pp. 1, 14, 24, cover top
right & 25; New Holland: pp. cover top left, 8, 10; Quicke/ALO: p. 13 bottom; RNLI: p. 29
(Mike Lang); Valtra: pp. 5, 11, 12, 15, 17, 22, 26, 28.

Printed in China

Franklin Watts is a division of Hachette Children's Books, an Hachette UK company.
www.hachette.co.uk

Contents

What are tractors?

Tractors are big machines. They do all kinds of work on the farm.

Farmers use tractors all of the time, so they must be able to work anywhere and in any weather. They can travel over rough, bumpy ground and through thick mud.

Tractors can do lots of jobs. They scoop up **manure**, carry bags of feed, spread **fertilizer** and pull heavy machinery across big fields.

Tractors help in emergencies too. They can be used to shovel snow or to pull people out of mud or floods when they get stuck!

Tractor fact!
In the United States more than four and a half million tractors are used in farming.

parts of the tractor

Look at all the different parts on the tractor!
Do you know what they are all for?

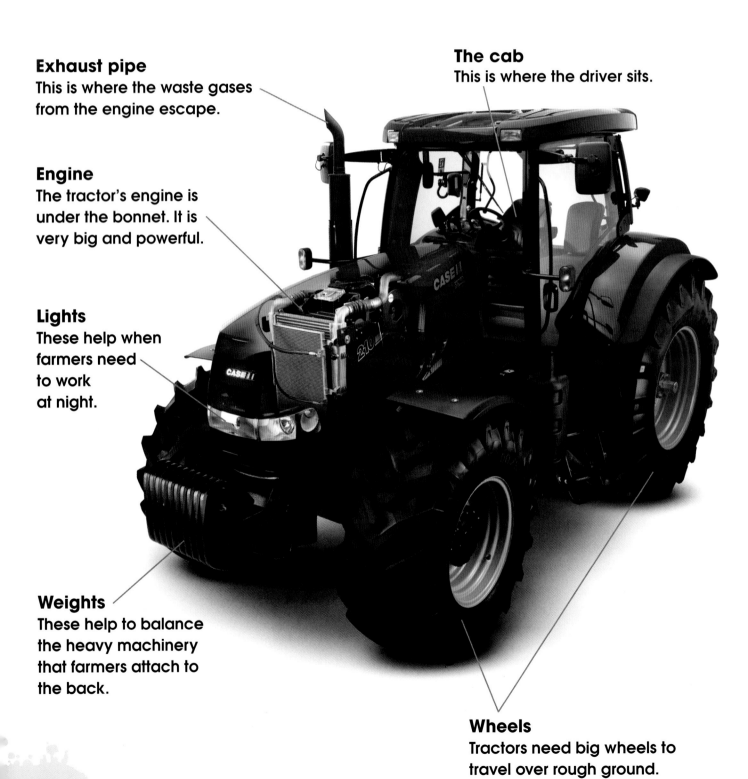

Exhaust pipe
This is where the waste gases from the engine escape.

Engine
The tractor's engine is under the bonnet. It is very big and powerful.

Lights
These help when farmers need to work at night.

Weights
These help to balance the heavy machinery that farmers attach to the back.

The cab
This is where the driver sits.

Wheels
Tractors need big wheels to travel over rough ground.

Wing mirror
This helps the farmer to see what is happening behind the tractor.

Indicators and brake lights
These tell people travelling behind the tractor what it is going to do.

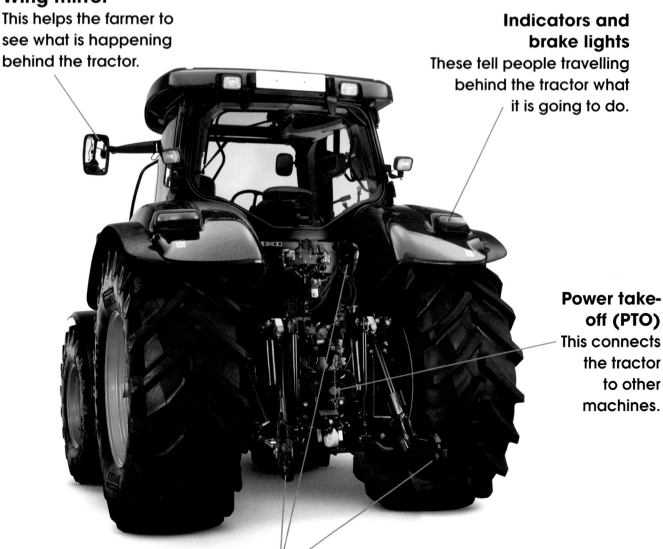

Power take-off (PTO)
This connects the tractor to other machines.

Three point linkage
This is used to attach other pieces of equipment to the tractor.

Wheels and tracks

Tractor wheels are covered by thick tyres. They have deep bumps on them called **lugs**. Lugs help the tractor to grip in slippery mud.

Lugs

The wheels are fixed on to **axles**. There is a front axle and a back axle. The front axle is connected to the steering wheel.

When the driver turns the steering wheel, it moves the front axle. This turns the front wheels.

Some tractors have tracks instead of wheels. The tracks are wide and long so the tractor's weight is spread out. This means that the tractor will not sink into soft ground.

Tracks

Tractor fact!
Tracks and tyres are made from very tough rubber.

Inside the tractor

The tractor driver sits in the cab. The cab is high up and there are steps to get up into it. The cab has big windows so that the driver can look out all around.

From the cab the driver can control the equipment attached to the front or back of the tractor.

Tractors need a lot of power to pull heavy machinery. This power comes from the big engine.

Engine

A tractor's engine needs fuel to make it work. Just like cars, different tractors use different types of fuel. Most tractors run on **diesel**.

Tractor fact!

New tractors are being developed that do not run on **petrol** or diesel. They will run on solar energy. This is energy from the Sun!

Lifting

A loader can be attached to the front of a tractor. This is a long arm with a hinge or joint in the middle. Different **implements** can be attached to the loader to do different jobs.

A bucket works like a big shovel. It can scoop up mud from one place and tip it out into a trailer.

Tractor fact!

Some loaders can lift things four metres into the air – they can reach the first floor windows of a house!

Another way to carry things is with a **grab**. This looks like a claw or pincer.

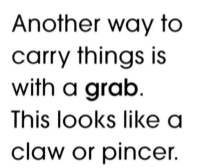

Bales

A **bale fork** can also be attached to the loader. This has prongs, like the fork you use to eat with. With the bale fork, the farmer can pick up and carry bales of hay.

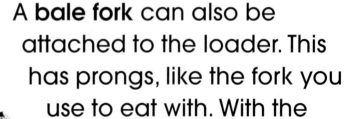

13

Tractors and trailers

Trailers fix on to the back of tractors. They can be very big and can be full of almost anything! It might be a **crop**, such as corn or potatoes, or animals, such as sheep or pigs.

Flat trailer

Farmers need different types of trailers for different jobs. Some are flat and can be piled high with bales.

Others are like big open boxes that can be filled with grain or vegetables that have been **harvested**.

Box trailer

Trailers can also be used to move animals around. These trailers have slots in the sides to let in the air. Some have two layers, or decks.

Tractor fact!
Some of the biggest trailers weigh 24 tonnes when they are full – that's the same as 24,000 bags of sugar!

Preparing the ground

Before farmers plant seeds, they must prepare the ground. They spread **slurry** on it using a slurry injector that is pulled along by a tractor.

Injectors

Then the hard earth is broken up with a plough. The tractor pulls the plough across the field. The plough digs up the earth and turns it over so that weeds and grass are buried.

Plough

Tractor fact!
In some places, ploughs and other pieces of farm equipment are pulled by horses or oxen.

Next, the farmer attaches a **harrow** to the tractor. This breaks up big lumps of earth.

Sowing seeds

When it is time to sow the seeds, farmers attach another piece of equipment to the tractor. This is called a seed drill.

The tractor pulls the seed drill across the field. The seeds fall down chutes from a container onto the ground.

When the seeds start to grow, the farmer sprays them with **nutrients**. These help crops to grow healthy and strong.

The sprayer is very wide. It is pulled along by the tractor.

Tractor fact!
In big fields farmers need to use very wide sprayers. Some are 24 metres wide!

Bringing in the harvest

At harvest time, the tractor and **combine harvester** work together. The combine harvester cuts the crop and separates the grain from the stalks.

The tractor pulls a trailer next to the combine harvester. The grain shoots out of a pipe at the top of the combine harvester and into the trailer.

The stalks are left on the field. The tractor pulls a baler around the field. It collects the dry stalks and squashes them into bales.

Bale

To harvest potatoes, the farmer uses a root crop harvester. The tractor pulls the root crop harvester across the field. It lifts potatoes out of the earth.

Tractor fact!
The biggest root crop harvester can dig up four rows of potatoes in one go!

21

Around the farm

There are lots of other jobs for tractors to do around the farm.

Farm fields must have strong fences and gates. To put in a big gatepost farmers can use a post driver.

Post driver

A post driver is attached to the back of a tractor. It holds a wooden post upright and a heavy weight is dropped on to the post to push it into the ground.

Farmers need to keep their hedges and **verges** neat and tidy. They can cut them using a trimmer. This is a cutting tool attached to a long arm that is joined to the tractor.

Tractor fact!
There are more than 50 different pieces of equipment that can can be fixed onto a tractor.

Small tractors

Tractors come in all shapes and sizes.

In orchards and **vineyards**, farmers need small tractors to move between the trees.

Some small tractors bend in the middle. They can move easily in tight places.

Tractor fact!
The smallest tractors have only two wheels. They are pushed along with handlebars. They have five horsepower engines – the biggest tractors have eight wheels and 600 horsepower engines!

Some small tractors are fitted with mowers.
These are used to cut the grass on golf
courses and in big gardens.

Farmers use a type of small tractor to get
around the farm. This is called a quad bike.
It is similar to a tractor, but much smaller.
It can only carry small loads.

The biggest tractors

Some big tractors have 'dual wheels'. This means another two wheels are attached to each axle, so they have eight wheels instead of four. This helps to spread their weight so that they don't sink into soft ground.

Tractor fact!
The biggest tractors can be 5 metres wide. They are too wide to travel on roads in the UK!

One company has invented a tractor with three axles – it has six wheels!

The very biggest tractors have a joint in the middle. This helps them to turn tight corners.

This is one of the biggest tractors. Its fuel tank holds 1,500 litres of fuel. That's enough to fill a normal car's fuel tank 25 times!

Special tractors

Tractors can be adapted, or changed, so that they can help with different jobs.

In the woods, foresters use special tractors to cut down and move trees. These tractors can move between trees and over the rough ground in a forest easily.

Tractor fact!
Some farming machines have been made that have legs instead of wheels or tracks. This means they can move around without damaging the forest floor.

Tractors have been made that can work in water. They are used to launch lifeboats from beaches into the sea. Water cannot get into the tractor, even if it is completely underwater.

The army also use specially adapted tractors. They cover them with armour so that they can work in dangerous places.

Tractor activities

History: Think of all the jobs that tractors do. How were these done years ago, before tractors were invented?

Geography: Tractors are used all over the world. Where do you think most tractors are used?

Art: Draw a design for a tractor. What will it be able to do?

Literacy: Write a story or poem about a tractor and the work that it does.

Science: Tractors are very powerful. How do you think you could measure a tractor's power?

Glossary

axles the rods that the wheels are attached to

bale fork a tool that can be attached to the tractor to lift bales

combine harvester a machine that cuts and removes the grain from crops

crop a plant that is grown in large amounts, usually for food

diesel a type of liquid fuel

fertilizer a substance that is put on land to help plants to grow

grab a tool that can be used to pick things up

harvest to cut or collect crops

implement a tool that can be connected to and powered by the tractor

lug a deep bump on a tyre

manure animal waste that is put on land to help plants to grow

nutrients substances that helps plants to grow

petrol a type of liquid fuel

power take-off a device that connects a tractor to another piece of equipment. It sends power from the tractor's engine to the equipment

slurry liquid animal waste

three point linkage three hitches, or hooks, that are used to attach equipment to the tractor

verge grassy patches of ground on the side of the road

vineyard farms where grapes are grown

Further information

Big Book of Tractors (John Deere), Heather Alexander, DK Publishing, 2007.

This is My Tractor (Mega Machine Drivers), Chris Oxlade, Franklin Watts, 2006.

Tractors (Big Machines), David and Penny Glover, Franklin Watts, 2007.

Tractors (Machines at Work), Caroline Bingham, DK Publishing, 2004.

Tractors (On the Go), David and Penny Glover, Wayland, 2007.

Tractors (Usborne Big Machines), Caroline Young, Usborne Books, 2003.

Index